Bible Study

7 SESSIONS FOR SMALL GROUP
AND PERSONAL USE

Matthew

Your Kingdom Come

Copyright © CWR, 2003.

Previously published by CWR as *Cover to Cover The Kingdom*, Waverley Abbey Resources, a trading name of CWR, Waverley Abbey House, Waverley Lane, Farnham, Surrey GU9 8EP, UK. Registered Charity No. 294387. Registered limited company No. 1990308. Reprinted 2007, 2008, 2009, 2013, 2017, 2023.

The right of Christine Leonard to be identified as the author of this work has been asserted by her in accordance with the Copyright, Designs and Patents Act 1988, sections 77 and 78.

All rights reserved. No part of this publication may be reproduced, stored in a retrieval system, or transmitted, in any form or by any means, electronic, mechanical, photocopying, recording or otherwise, without the prior permission in writing of Waverley Abbey Trust.

For a list of National Distributors, visit waverleyabbeytrust.org/distributors

Unless otherwise indicated, all Scripture references are from the NIV, New International Version® Anglicised, NIV® Copyright © 1979, 1984, 2011 by Biblica, Inc.® Used by permission. All rights reserved worldwide.

Other Bible translations:

NET Bible® copyright ©1996-2017 All rights reserved. Build 30170414 by Biblical Studies Press, L.L.C. Scripture taken from the New King James Version®. Copyright © 1982 by Thomas Nelson. Used by permission. All rights reserved.

Revised Standard Version of the Bible, copyright © 1946, 1952, and 1971 the Division of Christian Education of the National Council of the Churches of Christ in the United States of America. Used by permission. All rights reserved.

Every effort has been made to ensure that this book contains the correct permissions and references, but if anything has been inadvertently overlooked, the Publisher will be pleased to make the necessary arrangements at the first opportunity. Please contact the Publisher directly.

Concept development and editing by Waverley Abbey Trust.

Design and typesetting by Richard Lyall Design.

Printed and bound in the UK.

Paperback ISBN: 978-1-78951-450-6

Ebook ISBN: 978-1-78951-487-2

Contents

- 4   INTRODUCTION TO THE COVER TO COVER SERIES
- 6   ABOUT THE AUTHOR
- 7   INTRODUCTION
- 11   WEEK ONE
  Who is the King?
- 19   WEEK TWO
  Kingdom in Contention
- 27   WEEK THREE
  Radically Different Power and Authority – The Good News of the Kingdom
- 35   WEEK FOUR
  Growth – The Subversive Secret of the Kingdom
- 43   WEEK FIVE
  Upside-down Kingdom
- 51   WEEK SIX
  Kingdom Citizens' Responsibilities
- 59   WEEK SEVEN
  Laying Hold of the Kingdom
- 67   LEADER'S NOTES
- 79   DAILY GUIDE

About Cover to Cover

The *Cover to Cover* Bible Study Guides are a popular series helping individuals and groups to engage with the Bible and to dig deeper.

The first studies were produced in 2002 by Selwyn Hughes and now cover more than 80 different themes, characters and books of the Bible, and compiled by various writers and Bible teachers.

How to get the best from the studies

The *Cover to Cover* studies are designed to be either worked through individually or in a group. Whichever way you are using the study we encourage you to begin with prayer, asking God through His Holy Spirit to work in your life through these studies. Then trust that He will!

Do allow enough time for the questions and exercises, not rushing through but allocating time to focus on questions that raise specific challenges.

If you are studying as a group you may find our online resources useful. Here you will find some extra video content and copies of the daily guide to distribute to the members. Visit **wvly.org/c2ccv** to discover what is available.

In group discussions do make use of the leader's notes at the end of the study. Ensure that you give everyone in the group time to share and avoid allowing one person to dominate conversation.

Please feel free to adapt the material according to your group's needs. Trust that God is with you, leading you and helping each one of you draw closer to Him.

About the Author

Written by Chris Leonard

Chris Leonard leads many creative writing workshops and holidays and, with a degree in English and theology, she has 21 books published. Chris and her husband live in Surrey, England, have two grown-up children and three young grandchildren. She can be contacted at chrisleonardwriting.uk

Introduction

The Gospel of Matthew is so rich and full that we could be studying it for years but, for these seven weeks, we'll be concentrating on its main theme, which is 'the kingdom' and its King – Jesus. His very different way of exercising authority still has the power to change individuals' lives and societies in our troubled world.

Matthew's Gospel mentions the word 'kingdom' twice as often as any other book of the Bible. While Mark and Luke write of 'the kingdom of God', Matthew writes of 'the kingdom of heaven' (though a more literal translation would be 'the kingdom of the heavens'). Jesus came to make that realm visible to us – he brought some of heaven to earth.

Matthew's is, perhaps, the most Jewish of the Gospels and proclaims God as the true King of the Jews, then of the whole world. God intended Israel to live under His loving authority – an example to light the way back to God for other nations. Again and again Israel rebelled against God and finally most of their religious leaders rejected Jesus as their Messiah (Christ) whom God had sent.

As Matthew describes Jesus' life, death and resurrection, we can see God's authority working, not just in Israel but across every aspect of this material world where secular and religious despots, manipulators and false authorities appear to hold all the power. Matthew, most clearly of all the Gospel writers, shows Jesus as a kingly figure, who brought a bit of heaven, where God reigns in love and righteousness, to earth. The 'kingdom of heaven' continues to grow here wherever people like you and I agree to live by Jesus' power and under His authority.

Does the word 'kingdom' sound old-fashioned, even irrelevant to you, as if it belongs in some fairytale? Ask yourself: who exercises control, authority and power over you, your family, church, community, nation and the whole planet? In other words: who rules over what – and how does each exercise their control, for good or ill? Those questions, particularly ones about the abuse of power and control, fill news programming and countless everyday conversations as well as running right through the Bible, from Genesis to Revelation. Paul indicated that he preached nothing but 'Jesus Christ, and Him crucified' (1 Cor. 2:2), but Jesus Himself preached, prayed and lived out what He called 'the kingdom'. Matthew's Gospel makes very clear the difference between the 'kingdom of heaven' and all the authority that has gone so badly awry on earth.

According to this Gospel, the kingdom of heaven is a powerfully subversive secret, such as might be held by a resistance movement in wartime; it turns our thinking, our values and behaviour upside down. It contains the kind of surprises we should have learned to expect from a God who won't be put in boxes made with human understanding. The rewards cost everything, the battle's not over, but God is still inviting people to become citizens of His kingdom here on earth.

Before you read on

As we look at different aspects of control, power and authority in these studies, we'll be sampling from different bits of Matthew's Gospel – and including a few other parts of the Bible where they help illuminate the subject or the background and history of God's 'chosen people' as told in the Old Testament.

INTRODUCTION

Each week you'll find lots of Bible passages to read and more things to explore and questions to consider than is possible to cover in one evening. Every group is different and what will help one might confuse another. Choose carefully. Maybe read the passages in advance of the evening. And continue to explore some of the other bits God highlights for you in the days to come and/or at the suggestions in the Daily Guide.

I would urge you, before continuing with this book, to read through the whole of Matthew's Gospel in one sitting. Does that sound daunting? It shouldn't take much time – in my Bible it's a mere 40 pages long. Getting a feel for this Gospel as a whole will show you the complete picture, the whole story as told by Matthew, helping you to put into context the various extracts that we'll examine in more detail later. An alternative would be to prepare for your group study by having two or three sessions in which you gather to read Matthew aloud. Perhaps divide up the chapters between members of the group the week beforehand, giving everyone a chance to read their part with understanding. Whether you read alone or as a group, don't stop to question any difficult bits: instead let the story carry you on. If you do need to pause, pray back to God anything that has struck you in particular. God's Word will speak to us, if only we let it.

WEEK ONE
Who is the King?

Opening Exercise and Worship

Write or draw on slips of paper anything you associate with those who rule or have authority. Place them around a symbol of authority, such as a picture of a crown placed in the middle of the room. Then think of King Jesus. Take away any that no longer apply. Add more that do.

Use this as a basis for prayers and songs of praise and worship.

Bible Readings

- Matthew 1–2; 8; 21:1–11; 27:11,37
- 1 Samuel 8
- Psalm 89:3–4
- Daniel 2:44

Opening Our Eyes

We are looking at chapters in the Old Testament as well as Matthew, because it is the most Jewish Gospel and so we need some understanding of Jewish history and thought concerning kings, kingdoms and God. As you read passages familiar and unfamiliar, be asking yourselves: what kind of King is this; what kind of authority is He exercising?

Sometimes I wonder, had I lived in Jesus' time, would I have followed Him as King? All those miracles and healings were most attractive. Yet His radical teaching on the kingdom and His claim to be King of the Jews must have seemed bizarrely unreal, occurring under the rule of Rome and Herod.

Many Jews believed David's promised successor would overthrow the hated Romans and lend His support to the Temple priests. Jesus did neither. With no place to lay His head, let alone a palace, His only crown was made of thorns. How shockingly blasphemous to think the all-powerful God's anointed King would let Himself die in shameful agony at the hands of unjust secular and religious rulers!

Who is this King? Over what is He ruling? Those questions caused immense problems 2,000 years ago. That they remain relevant to millions of people (ultimately, to everyone) across the world today is, perhaps, the oddest thing of all.

Years beforehand, when Israel clamoured for a king, God was reluctant, even hurt. Wasn't He Himself their King, ruling in righteousness, faithfulness and power? How could they wish for better, when surrounding nations were demonstrating how horribly human kings can oppress their own people? But Israel was adamant. Sometimes God gives us what we want, if we plead long enough. Israel got the unstable Saul. After him came pathetically few 'good' kings, either from God's point of view

WHO IS THE KING?

or the people's — except for the great King David, flawed but described by God as a man after his own heart (Acts 13:22).

God had given a solemn promise that David's throne would last forever, his descendants would reign under God Himself for all time. Yet Israel — and her kings — kept rebelling against God. After the reforming punishment of exile, hope flickered again for a while but, for 200 years before Jesus came to earth, Jewish kings weren't descended from David at all. 'King' Herod wasn't even wholly Jewish. A usurping warlord, his power came through co-operation with the hated Roman occupiers of the Promised Land.

Matthew's Gospel begins with angels proclaiming the Saviour's supernatural arrival — yet here's a vulnerable, apparently illegitimate baby, a refugee fleeing the murderous authority of the counterfeit King Herod. Despite this and everything that happened afterwards, including His death, Jesus never once pulled back from His belief that, under God, He was King.

During His ministry, Jesus refused the normal trappings of power. Yet His attitude towards the law came with a king's authority. His stance towards everything, from storms to the sick and downtrodden, towards Scripture, foreigners, sin and Satan, reveals realms of authority extending way beyond kingship over God's chosen people. Jesus is King of everything in this universe in the same way as God is King. Remarkably, He remains in control right to (and through) death — because His authority came, not from people, but from God Himself. Vindicated, given all authority in heaven and on earth, His glorious rule of righteousness and love, faithfulness and peace, cannot fail to last forever.

Discussion Starters

1. The life of a really important person, in biblical times, would begin with a genealogy, tracing their ancestry. What can you find that is interesting – and odd – about King Jesus' ancestors in the start of Matthew's Gospel?

2. If you're a Christian you've put yourself under the rule of the strangest King in world history. What is the nature of the authority of Jesus (and God) and what does it mean in practical terms to you?

3. God's desire has always been to rule over the world in righteousness, mercy, justice, peace and salvation, so perhaps, even during His ministry on earth, Jesus wasn't such a strange King after all! Where can you see this special kind of kingship at work – in the Bible and today?

4. In Matthew 8 Jesus shows His kingdom authority. Was that kind of ministry special to Him and particularly necessary at that time, or can we expect to see such things as we follow Him today?

WHO IS THE KING?

5. What are your areas of influence and authority – do they sit within His kingdom authority, your own authority or someone else's?

a. Do you know anyone who combines humility and authority in a way that reminds you, however imperfectly, of Jesus – especially as He is portrayed in the passages from Matthew 21 and 27?

b. What can you learn from him or her as well as from Jesus?

c. How might these qualities combine to make your life, family, community, work and world more Christ-like?

Personal Application

The trouble with studying the Scriptures is that their implications are so radical and far-reaching. If we really grasped what the kingship of Christ means, if the whole world came under His kingship, imagine the difference it would make!

We all have control issues that affect our lives, and those of others. Who, rightly or wrongly, exercises authority over you, and over whom do you have some measure of control? Think about the question: 'What would Jesus do?' in the light of these things. How far can, or should, it apply? Where it does, and where following His way would mean change, how might that change be possible? Ask God to show you which areas of your life He doesn't have control over, and then ask Him to help you submit them fully to Him.

Seeing Jesus in the Scriptures

Her Majesty Queen Elizabeth II of the UK remains recognisable in various portraits but each painter portrayed something different of her personality. Just so, different aspects of Jesus are revealed in each of the four Gospels. Personally I find Matthew's the most difficult. As King, Jesus continued to reign through His trials, even from the cross. In Matthew we see less compassion and humanity, more challenging authority. Maybe that's why we don't just have one Gospel, but four. Writing this Study Guide, I've struggled with discouraging questions like, 'Have I even begun to understand what it means to follow King Jesus?' But His roles and titles include Shepherd, Saviour, Anointed One ('Christ' in Greek, 'Messiah' in Hebrew), Son of God, Son of Man, Suffering Servant, Lamb of God, Great High Priest... You might like to think how these (and more) relate to His kingship.

WHO IS THE KING?

Notes

WEEK TWO
Kingdom in Contention

Opening Exercise and Worship

If you find yourself in a (non-physical) conflict situation, what 'weapon' do you prefer to use? For example: write a letter, shout loudly, use 'sweet reason', get others on your side, crush with sarcasm, run and hide?

Now take time to read Psalm 45:4–9 and Matthew 12:15b–21. You might like to play some suitable music quietly in the background and perhaps light a candle as you spend a few quiet moments in meditative worship.

Bible Readings

- Matthew 4:1–17; 5:38–42; 12:22–28; 13:24–30,36–43; 21:33–44
- Daniel 7:9–27 (esp. vv13–14)

Opening Our Eyes

Jesus' mission was nothing less than establishing God's rule and reign on earth – that is, bringing the kingdom of heaven into present reality, here. And yet... wasn't God always King, reigning supreme over His creation? Well, yes... and no. That's the dramatic tension that fuels the whole sweep of the Bible's story. Yes, God is sovereign, His power absolute, always. He could have blasted rebellious humans and angels out of existence or forced them to obey, robot-like. But He didn't, even though that meant His reign of righteousness, peace and joy no longer always prevailed on this earth.

God chose another, extraordinary, way to begin to set His world aright again. He sent His Son. Jesus told us to 'turn the other cheek' (Matt. 5:39), which seems hard enough, but He did more, emptying Himself (Phil. 2:7, RSV), coming as a human being, quietly bringing God's rule to earth (Matt. 12:17–20). Through authoritative acts of creative grace, healing the sick, forgiving sin, throwing out demons, He brought the kingdom of God 'upon you' (12:28). Rejected and killed (21:33–44), vindicated by God at the resurrection, one day He will be fully honoured as King. For now, weeds still grow together with the wheat (Matt. 13). God's kingdom has come and, paradoxically, is still in contention while other kingdoms run in parallel.

Some strange apocalyptic visions in Daniel 7 are of the end times when, finally, the power of evil will be destroyed. Jesus' first coming did not bring the judgment day many had expected. John the Baptist was thinking of passages like Malachi 3:1–2 when he proclaimed Jesus coming with 'winnowing fork... in his hand, and he will clear his threshing-floor, gathering his wheat into the barn and burning up the chaff with unquenchable fire' (Matt. 3:12). No wonder John urged, 'Repent, for the kingdom of heaven has come near' (3:2). John prepared the way for Jesus, but I wonder if he understood that Jesus was coming not to destroy, but to save? Far bigger issues than temporary rule over parts of the earth were at stake: the fate of all created beings – mind, body and spirit – eternally. Perhaps that is why God set about re-establishing His kingdom in such an extraordinary, creative, painful way.

Jesus was led out to the desert immediately before His earthly ministry began. The temptations described in Matthew 4 concern the way in which He would achieve His purpose of re-establishing God's kingdom on earth. The Roman Empire ruled by might and fear – and also through 'bread and circuses' (food and fearsomely entertaining spectacles). Jesus rejected those methods as He rejected the first two temptations. He would not work spectacular magic tricks or give the people what they wanted in order to win them. With the third temptation, Satan overplayed his hand, as he often does. The kingdoms of the world might have been in contention but they've never belonged wholly to the father of lies! Had God's Son worshipped Satan at that point, things might have been different, but of course such a thing was absurd. Jesus had full authority to send him packing.

After His time in the wilderness, Jesus began to preach – and the Galileans who had been living in darkness and the shadow of death saw, not destruction, but 'a great light' (Matt. 4:16). The kingdom of heaven was indeed near – and it's the grace of God that leads to repentance. True repentance means turning around and living under the rule of a new King!

Discussion Starters

1. Don't spend time trying to understand the details in Daniel 7 but consider, what does it mean to you – what difference might it make – that Jesus, the Son of Man (as well as of God) *is* on the throne in heaven?

2. We've only to watch the news to see the clash of the kingdoms of good and evil in this world. You know the end of the great cosmic story before it has fully unfolded. What difference does that knowledge make to the way that you live now? What difference do you think it made to Jesus?

3. Can you give instances where Scripture has helped you in situations where you have faced temptation or evil? What else helps when you find yourself in the front line of conflict or being deflected from the course that you know God wants you to take?

4. What do you find the most remarkable about the way in which God chose to re-establish His kingdom? Can you learn anything that might apply when things get in an unholy mess in your workplace, family or neighbourhood?

KINGDOM IN CONTENTION

5. What difference has Jesus' (first) coming made to justice and the hope of nations (Matt. 12:18–21) in this world? Do you see yourself and other Christians as having any part to play in that?

6. When you see kingdoms clash openly, how do you know who is on which side? (Matt. 12:22–28).

7. What is the kingdom way to resist evil and oppression? Setting oppressed people free was part of Jesus' declared kingdom mission (Luke 4:17–21), yet His words in Matthew 5:38–42 seem to give the opposite advice. What is going on here? What's the right, 'kingdom thing' to do if our children are bullied at school, for example? Should we support things like the United Nations' charter of human rights?

Personal Application

It's a huge and difficult question — how can we oppose evil in a godly way? What can you learn from the way God acts when kingdoms are in contention? Having done this study, would you want to change the 'weapon' you chose during the opening exercise? If so (and you change it in real life too!) that's repentance. Repentance is not something to be ashamed of, but good news — it's what happens when Jesus and His kingdom draw near!

Seeing Jesus in the Scriptures

We have already been focusing on Jesus throughout our study, but you might like to consider the huge impact that Jesus had on someone who wasn't a Christian. Gandhi, while reading the Bible, understood that Jesus had remedies for the injustices that troubled him. Wondering about changing his religion in order to follow this amazing teacher more closely, Gandhi went along to a church in London. They turned him away, telling him to worship with his own people. Concluding that Christians failed to live out Christ's teaching, he remained in the Hindu religion. However, he decided to follow the way in which Jesus brought in the kingdom — by meeting injustice and oppression with non-violent resistance. By a mixture of suffering, service, fasting and growing moral authority, plus a little help from his friends, Mahatma Gandhi won independence for a 'kingdom in contention' — India. Like any other human being, Gandhi was by no means all good, but his response to the Bible poses a real challenge to us. While not a Christian, he nonetheless not only saw Jesus in the Scriptures, but followed His seemingly strange ways — with amazing results.

Notes

WEEK THREE
Radically Different Power and Authority – The Good News of the Kingdom

Opening Exercise and Worship

Ask everyone to say, briefly, what news item from the past week has affected them the most and why.

Think for a moment – what in particular about Jesus strikes you as good news at the moment. Then pray, silently or out loud, thanking Him for that specific thing.

Bible Readings

- Matthew 5:1–12, 17–22; 6:33; 7:13–14; 9:1–10:8 (esp. 9:12–13; 10:5–8); 11:2–6
- Hosea 6:1–6

Opening Our Eyes

Every day we see a mixture of good news and bad. The media bombards us mainly with bad news. But 'gospel' means good news. That's what Jesus came to announce. He didn't just preach the cross (He also lived that!), He preached – and demonstrated, very practically – the good news of the kingdom. As He said to John the Baptist, the coming of the kingdom was evident in that the blind saw, the lame walked, lepers were cured, the deaf heard, the dead were raised and the poor were hearing good news (Matt. 4-6)! The power of life in Christ Jesus was defeating the power of sin, sickness, lies and death – defeating the usurping enemy's strongholds.

Because of who He is and the way He rules, the coming of God's kingdom is very good news indeed. Imagine a world where everyone lived under His rule and reign, wouldn't it be like, well, heaven? Certainly it would be a lot more like heaven than living on earth actually is! Living under His rule may start as a narrow, more difficult path but, because He is a good Shepherd, a good King, it leads to a broad place, right relationships, to life in all its fulness (John 10:10) – and not just after death! Look at Jesus, who had nothing, yet brought such riches, whose unimaginable pain made joy possible again, whose giving away of everything made Him (and us) ready to receive far more.

The impression often given by the media is that Christians are miserable, bigoted and repressed – at best living in cloud cuckoo land, at worst the cause of deep psychological damage to helpless children and weak-minded people. Yet statistics have shown that Christians are happier and experience significantly less divorce and mental illness than do the rest of the population in the UK. Of course we get plenty of things wrong. Living under Jesus' rule was never going to be painless or easy – this good news is far from glib. Re-reading Matthew's Gospel, though, I found myself thinking – have I

RADICALLY DIFFERENT POWER AND AUTHORITY

ever seen anyone living in the way Jesus told us to? Losing our lives, healing the sick, raising the dead, keeping every commandment? I honestly don't think I have – and I myself am a million miles away. Jesus' words are so challenging that all I can say is, 'I – we – need His grace so much.' It's not cheap grace, but the Beatitudes (blessed are the poor in spirit, those who mourn etc) seem to be saying they are 'good news for those who know they are needy'. We're not going to get there on our own. One phrase Jesus repeats in this Gospel is a quote from Hosea 6:6, 'I desire mercy, not sacrifice' (Matt. 9:13). This 'kingdom thing' isn't about religion, it's about attitude, it's about caring for others, it's about doing those things we see the Father doing, it's about knowing God and being known. The best news of all is that He knows us – and still loves us. It's interesting that, in context, Hosea wrote, 'after two days he will revive us, on the third he will restore us' (Hos. 6:2). Israel had been turning away to do wrong, breaking the covenant with God, needing, as we need, His huge wells of love and His power of resurrection life.

Discussion Starters

1. What is it about your life that communicates some aspect of the good news that Jesus brings? What is it about your church that does the same? Is there a difference between preaching the gospel and bringing the kingdom near, which is what Jesus asked of His disciples in Matthew 10:5–8?

2. How can we live out the kind of righteousness that means we're part of the good news of the kingdom to others? How can we access the power to live this kingdom way?

3. God had chosen Israel to spread His light to the nations. When that didn't happen, Jesus chose twelve disciples (echoing the twelve tribes of Israel) for the same mission – to be continued by us, the Church. Matthew and the other eleven disciples had not long been called when Jesus sent them out to proclaim and be good news of the kingdom. What do you make of this? Has the Church in materially richer, less persecuted and 'needy' parts of the world lost (or sold) out on this aspect of being good news?

RADICALLY DIFFERENT POWER AND AUTHORITY

4. Look again at Matthew 9:20–22. Do we, like the Pharisees (see Matt. 23:13), ever shut people whom we consider unsavoury out of the kingdom – perhaps because we are afraid that they will contaminate us? Or do we let them come close and let God's cleansing, healing life flow through us to touch them?

5. 'I desire mercy and not sacrifice.' How might that phrase affect your personal, and your church's, relationship with God – and with other people?

6. Have you found it to be true that, if you seek God's kingdom and righteousness first, 'all these things' (our material needs) will be given to you as well (Matt. 6:33)? How does the cost of living in God's kingdom tie up with the good news?

Personal Application

As Christians, we pray that God's kingdom will come. How are you helping bring in the kingdom of God? Not just in 'churchy' ways but maybe by being good news at work – perhaps in the business world or as a health worker, or by your involvement with individual children or vulnerable adults. You may be building a family and perhaps a sense of community in your neighbourhood or children's school. You may influence people more widely through politics, the arts or media. Think about the possibilities, the difficulties and opportunities for being good news that lie before you. Ask others in the group to pray for you and pray for them.

Seeing Jesus in the Scriptures

Take encouragement in the fact that Jesus, having 'emptied himself' walked this earth as a human being. This was the way that He brought in the kingdom, not fully, but enough to affect many lives and places two millennia later. He doesn't ask us to do anything that He hasn't done Himself!

Notes

WEEK FOUR
Growth – The Subversive Secret of the Kingdom

Opening Exercise and Worship

If you are meeting somewhere with a kitchen, bring a recipe, ingredients and equipment for making bread. Start it off as people arrive, and let everyone have a go with the mixing and kneading as you follow the process through its various stages. Watch how the yeast makes the dough rise, feel its stickiness and, later on, enjoy the smell. There are alternative suggestions to bread-making in the Leader's Notes (see page 72) but, whether or not you make bread, some groups might want to bring the elements of the Lord's Supper and share them together at the end of the evening.

Bible Readings

- Matthew 5:38–48; 6:1–8; 13:11–23,31–33,44–46
- Acts 2:36–47

Opening Our Eyes

Have you ever wondered about God – why, though infinitely big and powerful, He seems to like starting things really small? He designed forest trees to start with seeds that can get lost or lie around for years, waiting to germinate, then grow, oh so slowly. Even more strange, He sent His Son to earth not as a man, or boy, or even a newborn baby – He sent a 'seed' to grow in the womb of a young, unmarried girl. He set about establishing His kingdom without using legions of fighting angels, prestigious palaces or multimedia marketing presentations. As Jesus proclaimed His message, died and rose again, comparatively few people on earth met Him or heard about His kingdom. Far from proclaiming Himself King or Messiah, He'd urge people to keep His identity secret. He even thanked God that He had 'hidden these things from the wise and learned, and revealed them to little children' (Matt. 11:25). A smattering of unlikely souls guessed who He was, but few really understood; several ran away, one or two betrayed Him.

Jesus spoke of bread-making, which takes a long while. Bread made in haste, like in the drama of the first Passover, has to be made without yeast. To get proper bread, people or trees you have to wait! Meanwhile, as dough rises in a warm, dark place, as hidden cells multiply in a womb or underground, little appears to be happening, though fundamental changes are taking place in secret. Particularly in today's world, where we hate waiting for anything, God's thoughts are not our thoughts; His ways don't conform to ours (see Isa. 55:8–9)!

'Is Napoleon's hat still in Ploumanac'h?' These strange words can be found written in French on a plaque in Brittany. They celebrate a wartime coded radio message, sent from Britain just before the D-Day landings, to activate local French resistance against the Nazis. God's kingdom on earth, though fully operative in the Person of Jesus, started off in a similar scenario – a small, subversive secret, in hostile territory. How vulnerable He was, the rightful yet uncrowned King living in usurped territory, teaching about the kingdom! The more people understood who He was, the more His life would be at risk, perhaps before His ministry was complete. It nearly spelt disaster when the Magi asked Herod for the 'one who has been born king of the Jews' (Matt. 2:2). When the crowd in Matthew 21 recognised their gentle King coming to Jerusalem on a donkey, as their prophet Zechariah foretold, they proclaimed Him 'Son of (King) David'. The shocking secret was out properly and soon Jesus was raised up and proclaimed 'King of the Jews' – on the cross.

After He rose, ascended and sent the Holy Spirit, things changed. Jesus gave His followers (including us) authority and responsibility to spread the good news of His kingdom, worldwide (Matt. 28:18–20). The disciples proclaimed His message openly and thousands responded. But then came intense persecution and the need for more care again. Jesus would never have His kingdom spread by force (though too many who followed Him have mistakenly believed He would). In many parts of the world, the Kingship of Jesus remains highly dangerous. More Christians lived in the past 100 years than ever before; more Christians died for their faith. Remember to pray for, and honour, them. Eventually, of course, the kingdom will be established and shouted from every rooftop for, when God fully declares His glory, every knee will bow to the King of kings (Rom. 14:11).

Discussion Starters

1. In the readings from Matthew 13 Jesus was saying, 'The kingdom of heaven is like...' Have you seen those kingdom ways and principles at work in your own lives? How do you cope with waiting for God's 'interesting' timing? What experience do you have of investing in kingdom things that may seem foolish?

2. For over 2,000 years Christians have prayed, 'Your kingdom come' – without seeing the full answer. But what changes has this 'subversive secret' brought to our world? What transformations has it brought to your life and the lives of those with whom you're in contact? And what transformations in particular are you longing and praying for now?

3. Jesus didn't go around blurting out His message. He taught using parables – stories and pictures that spoke to 'those who had ears to hear'. Those who had eyes to see understood who He was from His actions. Does any of this conflict with Jesus' commands to keep our good actions secret (6:1–8)? What stories, pictures and actions might communicate with those whose hearts are open today? Before discussing this, you might like to spend some time listening to God!

GROWTH – THE SUBVERSIVE SECRET OF THE KINGDOM

4. Some of Jesus' hardest teaching comes in Matthew 5:38–48 – few resistance movements have urged love for enemies! You might like to consider the effects of some that have come near, whether Christian or not, such as struggles led by Gandhi, Martin Luther King, Archbishop Desmond Tutu…

5. Stories of Christians putting Jesus' teaching into practice have often come from areas of real trauma, where, through great suffering, the kingdom did advance and evil was defeated. Do you know of any? Do you believe – and follow – Jesus' teaching in any areas where you sometimes feel oppressed?

Personal Application

There's something exciting about sharing a secret. And now that most people in developed nations know Jesus perhaps chiefly as a swear word, and haven't a clue about His kingdom, what a secret to share! Can you get excited again about this amazing secret of the King and His 'kingdom of the heavens' on earth? Who can you share that excitement with? What 'seeds' has God given you? Where does He want you to sow them?

Seeing Jesus in the Scriptures

If you've never done this before, take time to read portions of the Old Testament, keeping a note of wherever you find the subversive secret of Jesus. He's there for those who have eyes to see.

Before you break bread together, you might like to read the story of the Lord's Supper in Matthew 26:17–30. As you meditate on this, consider also Jesus' teaching about yeast and the subversive secret of the kingdom: 'Take and eat; this is my body' (v28).

GROWTH – THE SUBVERSIVE SECRET OF THE KINGDOM

Notes

WEEK FIVE
Upside-down Kingdom

Opening Exercise and Worship

Ask everyone to think of an example of how life has treated them unfairly – this might be to their advantage or disadvantage. When such things happened, psalmists would communicate with God about them, in psalms of praise or lament. Take ten minutes and each write your own short personal psalm about an unfair incident. Read some of these out as an act of worship.

Bible Readings

- Matthew 8:1–13; 19:13–20:16; 21:12–17,28–32; 22:1–10; 23:13–15

Opening Our Eyes

'It's not fair!' That, according to my mother, was my cry every afternoon when I came home from school. Some child who'd done wrong had got away with it, maybe even been rewarded, while the ones who worked hard had been given even more to do. The thing is, we could be tempted to say that God isn't fair, either; that Jesus isn't fair. He even turned logic upside down – kings who die don't normally stay kings, let alone get resurrected and promoted and destined to have all creation under their feet. Is the kingdom fair? It simply isn't fair, is it, that a worker gets paid the same amount for an hour as for a whole day? It may seem unfair to us but it was totally just. In the kingdom, fairness is turned utterly upside down – and that is just as well for us! We wouldn't even be in this kingdom if the King himself hadn't loved us rebels enough to die for us. How upside down, how 'unfair' is that?! The gift of salvation is not about fairness but grace, which is freely available for all.

Even so, it's hard for us to understand just how upside-down Jesus' version of the kingdom appeared to the people who first encountered it. To them it was inconceivable that the kingdom should belong to such 'insignificant' beings as children, Gentiles or those disfigured by obvious sin or ailment. Everyone knew that God's favour rested most with Jewish men who kept His law – He'd bless them with riches and power. Jesus affronted the status quo by saying it would be incredibly hard for rich people to enter His kingdom and that many who were first here would be last there. Everyone knew that lepers were not only dangerous but ceremonially unclean. They weren't allowed near the Temple, but Christ touched them, welcomed them and healed them. Everyone knew that God loves righteousness and hates sin. Yet Jesus announced that obvious sinners, who hurt other people by the jobs they did – the prostitutes and cheating,

Roman-pleasing tax-collectors — would enter the kingdom of heaven ahead of upright religious types. Utterly shocking, isn't it?

It was more than shocking; it was extremely confrontational. The power-base of the Temple was arranged in courts that progressively excluded more and more people. The disabled or ceremonially unclean weren't allowed anywhere near, Gentiles and women were kept well to the exterior, priests and Levites were allowed a little closer than religious laymen but only the high priest could enter the Holy of Holies and he only once a year. The expensive and complicated system of sacrifices excluded the poor. Jesus, however, not only overturned the money-changers' tables in the Temple courts, He healed the blind and the lame there. Children greeted Him there, shouting, 'Hosanna to the Son of David!' No wonder He was in trouble with the Jewish authorities who had their own system working very nicely, thank you!

Early in His ministry it looked like Jesus had been sent to Israel, the people God had chosen to be a light to the nations. The Roman centurion's faith came as a real eye-opener — this man trusted and understood His authority, while religious Jews were hostile and said His power came from demons! In rejecting Jesus, the kingdom was taken from them (Matt. 21:43). It's interesting that most of Jesus' interaction with non-Jews comes towards the end of this Gospel.

Jesus knew His Father. He knew that He desired 'mercy not sacrifice', kingdom life not religion. And it was that grace that turned everything upside down.

Discussion Starters

1. Where are the kind of individuals who became kingdom people in Jesus' day? Are the prostitutes, the perverts and cheats, the marginalised, the prisoners, immigrants and mentally ill in your area becoming kingdom people? If so, are they welcome in your church? What changes of attitude and arrangements does that entail, not least regarding important matters of safeguarding? If social outcasts are showing no signs of flocking into the kingdom, what do you think is wrong and what can you do – and pray – about it?

2. Do you see the kingdom of heaven as belonging to the children in your church (Matt. 18:1–5)? What do you learn from them?

UPSIDE-DOWN KINGDOM

3. What is your attitude towards those who are intelligent, well-off and well-groomed? Be honest: do you value them more than others? Jesus often turned accepted ways of looking at people on their heads. What changes need to happen to our vision, if we're to see people through His eyes?

4. People in Jesus' time couldn't really cope with God's astounding grace. Do you find it difficult today? If we accepted His grace fully, what difference might it make to our lives?

5. Religious leaders of Jesus' day (as well as plenty throughout church history) 'shut the door of the kingdom of heaven in men's faces' (Matt. 23:13) and established something very different from God's rule of 'justice, mercy and faithfulness' (v23). How can we, as individual Christians and as the Church, ensure we are building God's kingdom and not one where we are in charge?

Personal Application

I have a foreign friend whose job is very demanding and difficult. She works full-time with adults who have the most profound learning, as well as physical, disabilities. 'Oh how I love them!' she emailed me today. 'God is so mercy [sic], always I ask myself, do I deserve such happiness and goodness?' She is living, quite naturally, in God's upside-down kingdom, proving the truth of its seemingly reversed natural laws. Those who give will receive. Those who lose their lives do find them. Those who love the unlovely do find the deepest love and joy of all. My friend is living almost as differently as someone would need to on a planet without gravity. Sometimes I think I'm a long way from entering fully into this upside-down kingdom of Jesus. How about you? Are there areas where God's grace has enabled you to live 'upside down'? Are there changes that you need to make in your daily life in order to live in this way?

Seeing Jesus in the Scriptures

Although Jesus turned accepted thinking – and life itself – upside down, people needn't have been taken by surprise. Right through the Old Testament God's heart is very much for the poor and marginalised, as well as for all nations. You only need to look at the 'suffering servant' passages in Isaiah 42:1–9; 49:1–9a; 50:4–11; 52:13–53:12; 61:1–4, to see that they foretell a Saviour very different from the one many of Jesus' countrymen were expecting.

UPSIDE-DOWN KINGDOM

Notes

WEEK SIX
Kingdom Citizens' Responsibilities?

Opening Exercise and Worship

Ask everyone to think of a time when they lived in a community, even if it was only for a week's holiday. What specifically did they find good, and what difficult, about it?

Welcome the King among the community of your group now as you worship Him together, each contributing something, if possible – maybe a Bible verse, words from a worship song or poem, a prayer, even an object such as a flower or a picture that speaks about something of God that is special to you.

Bible Readings

- Matthew 7:17–23; 16:13–19; 18:21–35; 19:12
- Judges 17:6; 21:25

Opening Our Eyes

I was listening to a psychologist on the radio one day who was explaining how young teenagers 'need' to experiment to find the kind of sexuality with which they 'feel comfortable'. Those who've not experienced a variety of sexual relations by fifteen 'feel odd' apparently – which, 'might be a bit of a pressure, since individuals mature at different rates'. I found myself longing for some kingdom righteousness, for love and care rather than competitive self-gratification, for sex to be restored to the wonderful, loving, intimate thing the Creator-King always intended it to be.

At church one Sunday, a teacher thanked God for safety on a school trip he'd led. 'These days most teachers think you're mad to lead a trip,' he explained. 'The consequences are so dire should anything go wrong.' I remember, from decades ago, eyes blazing from my television screen – eyes of grief-stricken parents whose teenagers had wandered off while on a school trip and died in a tragic accident. Desperate for someone to blame, the parents' agony, deepened over the months into bitterness, ultimately helped the current generation to be deprived of good things. A caring paediatrician, under huge pressure of time, misses for once diagnosing an incredibly rare condition; when angry parents complain and sue for millions of public money all the training and skills of that doctor become unavailable to thousands of other families. In these circumstances I feel myself longing for kingdom ways. Forgiveness may be the hardest thing, but the alternatives are terrible, both for individuals and society.

In most of the developed world today the individual is king and everyone does what is 'right in [their] own eyes' as Judges 21:25 is translated in the NKJV. That easy-road mindset still affects us as Christians. Do you, like me, sometimes feel, 'Well, God's good, I love knowing Him – but Christians are driving me mad!' Do you, like me, find yourself upsetting those people you

KINGDOM CITIZENS' RESPONSIBILITIES?

love the most? 'Deepening my relationship with God' is well and good, but if it's true that God is King, then we are citizens of His righteous kingdom and need to demonstrate that His heart is for the community.

Real kingdom community is very different from the norm since it's what God thinks that counts, rather than the opinions of members. A 'kingdom community' doesn't equate to the church/es in any one place either. It's far wider than that. 'The kingdom of God is among you' wherever God's people, empowered by the Spirit, spread the ways of the kingdom.

The Romans' highly organised, powerful armies conquered nation after nation. God's kingdom doesn't work that way. But I was fascinated to hear archaeologists explaining that the 'Roman villa' they were excavating probably belonged, not to ancient Italians, but to people whose well-off families had lived in Britain long-term. They had decided central heating and baths were preferable to your average smoky hut and adapted to the Roman way of life. Do our Christian communities attract people, and convince them that the kingdom way of life is good? Do we, behaving in a kingdom way in our neighbourhood or workplace, make it more like the kingdom of God? Do we bring hope to the marginalised and health to the sick in heart, spirit or body? Revising this book 20 years after first writing it, I thank God for all the Christian initiatives I can see that have sprung up to make a vital difference.

Sometimes Christians emphasise sin and give the impression that 'living righteously' is about not doing outwardly wrong things. It's far more than that. It's about doing right, doing 'the will of the Father', who loves all of His children, whether or not they know Him. He is very concerned that we treat each other well, especially any who are vulnerable, and that concern hasn't changed in thousands of years – because it is the essence of His kingdom. To love and know the King empowers us to love His kingdom!

Discussion Starters

1. What, in practical terms, does it mean to you, not 'just' to have a relationship with Jesus but to be in His kingdom? Are you involved in a community beyond church walls? Are you helping to make it be more like the kingdom of heaven?

2. Imagine Jesus moves into your neighbourhood and starts going to your church. What might change in the way people treat one another?

3. Who are kingdom people and what makes us distinct as a community – or communities? What are our roles? What are the practical implications of Jesus' prediction that 'bad eggs' (fish/fruit) would remain in the mix until the end of the age?

KINGDOM CITIZENS' RESPONSIBILITIES?

4. The way people use and abuse such things as trust, money, sex and power affects everyone. How can we live in a distinctively kingdom way, salting our communities with goodness, rather than being judgmental and appearing 'holier than thou'?

5. If kingdom people are given power from God, on earth and in heaven, how do we use it – especially corporately? What are the dangers and opportunities?

6. Who, 2,000 years on, has the keys of the kingdom? What does it mean to bind and loose on earth and in heaven? What part, if any, do you have in that?

Personal Application

Where does God want you to operate primarily – in the church or in extending His kingdom? In which do you spend most of your time? Listen to Him – in the light of kingdom teaching might He be calling you to use some of your free time differently? Maybe if you feel some change is needed you could share that with the group another time and receive some prayer.

Seeing Jesus in the Scriptures

Jesus used the Rabbinical technique of hyperbole (extreme exaggeration) in some of his sayings, in order to convey the absolute importance of key kingdom principles such as forgiveness and hearing and obeying God's will. To us this can seem pretty scary. Remember that He also said, 'My yoke is easy and my burden is light' (Matt. 11:28–30). He welcomed despised, sinful, broken adults and bouncy children with runny noses. Remember that He loves you so much that He died for you. He rose again that you might know the power of that resurrection to do some of the seemingly impossible things He appears to be asking in this upside-down kingdom of His. And remember, no community is perfect this side of heaven – the community Jesus built around Himself certainly wasn't. All the better for rubbing a few rough edges off each other as we are made ready for eternal life in the kingdom of heaven!

KINGDOM CITIZENS' RESPONSIBILITIES?

Notes

WEEK SEVEN
Laying Hold of the Kingdom

Opening Exercise and Worship

Can you think of something that might be here but not here? Maybe, for example, it exists in some (different?) way in the past, present and future. What tensions might be caused when things don't exist yet in the form that we (and God) would like?

A string held in tension may either snap or be plucked or bowed by a skilled musician to produce a beautiful note. Bring your tensions and pain into God's presence now. Allow Him to take them; He might just turn them into beautiful 'music'.

Bible Readings

- Matthew 5:17–20; 11:11–12; 24:14; 25:1–13, 31–46; 28:16–20.

Opening Our Eyes

I lie face down, watching a kingdom below me whose inhabitants live, move and have their being differently from anything in my experience. Take breathing – they extract oxygen from water; I watch from the upper surface of their kingdom thanks to a snorkel leading to the air. Their watery kingdom covers four-fifths of the earth – yet relatively few land-dwellers have seen beneath its surface. For a start, we have to be able to swim, or at least trust the water will hold us as we relax in this improbable position.

The paragraph above would be my contribution to a brainstorm on 'the kingdom of heaven is like…'. The number of times Jesus repeated that phrase indicates that it's hard for us to understand. The kingdom's real, here and now – yet most people remain unaware of it. The kingdom with God in charge and the realm where man or Satan has assumed control exist at the same time, like land and sea – 'parallel universes' complete with different laws and ways of living. To transfer from one to the other means seizing hold – buying a snorkel and learning to swim, or seeking, then buying into, God's kingdom, submitting your life to Christ's rule and reign, trusting utterly in Him.

Religious Jews repeated the Kaddish prayer daily, 'May he establish his kingdom in your lifetime.' John the Baptist prepared the way, declaring it 'near' (Matt. 3:1–2) and Jesus also proclaimed its nearness at the start of His ministry (4:17). Things changed forever in the next verses, however, for that is when He called His first disciples. This wasn't the old kingdom of Israel that Jesus was establishing. His brand-new kingdom needed subjects and began when three fisherman changed utterly the way they lived, 'left the boat and their father and followed [Jesus]' (4:22). In the same way, the kingdom of God came when Jesus threw out demons by the Spirit of God (12:28), leaving the delivered people free to follow Jesus' rule

LAYING HOLD OF THE KINGDOM

and reign, rather than Satan's. No wonder religious Jews were shocked – this was hardly the kingdom they expected!

Most action in the Gospels occurs before the resurrection of course. But that's when things really change because that's when the Father ratifies Jesus' righteousness, His kingly authority. Afterwards Jesus says to His disciples, 'All authority in heaven and on earth has been given to me. Therefore go and make disciples of all nations...' 'Therefore' carries an enormous weight!

This Gospel asks a key question: whose is the kingdom of heaven? Jesus says that 'forceful people lay hold of it' (Matt. 11:12, NET). People don't drift in because they attend Church or are born into a particular nation – they need to seek the kingdom, buying into something that costs everything and to 'find the narrow gate'. The kingdom hasn't yet fully come. Not everyone has submitted to Christ's rule, though in the future we know that there will be a final judgment, and that every knee will bow. Until then there's a very real struggle. Kingdom people follow Jesus in finding the Spirit's power to be wise and prepared, righteous and compassionate. They pray and preach the gospel of the kingdom in the whole world; 'and then the end will come' (24:14). Then those 'who are blessed by my Father' will 'take your inheritance, the kingdom prepared for you since the creation of the world' (25:34).

Discussion Starters

1. Bearing in mind Matthew 5:17–20, how can we 'enter' let alone 'lay hold of' the kingdom of heaven, and what impact does the 'therefore' in Matthew 28:19 have on your laying hold of the kingdom?

2. What are the implications of trying to exist in both kingdoms?

3. Wrong interpretations of Matt. 11:12 may well have contributed to disasters for the kingdom such as the Crusades or the Conquistadors' forcible baptisms, so what do you think Jesus meant by, 'The kingdom of heaven has been forcefully advancing, and forceful men lay hold of it'? (Some translate this phrase in an even stronger way – 'violently/violent'.) Are there areas where He is calling you to use His kingdom authority more 'forcefully'? If so, what other kingdom principles might prevent this turning into a set-back for the kingdom?

4. Many religious Jews in Jesus' time were praying and longing for the Messiah and making huge efforts to keep to the letter of God's law, yet they failed to recognise Jesus or to enter into His kingdom. Bearing in mind 25:1–13, how can we be wiser and more prepared than they were?

5. Religion can mean making God after our own image and looking godly as we strain to do what we think He wants. In the light of 25:31–46, are we really following God or could our very religion or self-centredness cause us to go astray?

6. Why is it vital that the gospel of the kingdom be preached in the whole world (24:14), to all nations (the word means people-groups) before 'the end' – the second coming of the Son of Man? What part do you have to play in showing other people-groups some of the good things you've found through, and about, Jesus?

7. The 'good news' in this Gospel comes salted with plenty of judgment. Why do you think that is? Does strong judgment sit easily with your picture of Jesus?

Personal Application

If I love and respect someone, then to see their will flouted, their name degraded, the things they've made and people they care for trashed will hurt. And in some ways the more we love God and long to see His kingdom come, the more we'll find this world painful, as He must find it painful. Sometimes we may need to acknowledge that, to Him and to one another. We need to encourage one another to see His hope beyond daily news of fresh horrors, to fix our eyes on His beauty amid the ugliness, to rekindle our faith that His kingdom's winning through is not in doubt – and that He trusts us with parts to play as He achieves victory!

Seeing Jesus in the Scriptures

Pray the Lord's Prayer, reading it in unison from Matthew 6:9–13, then praise Him for ways in which you have seen His kingdom come. Pray for those who are especially feeling the tension between two kingdoms, or are in the 'front line' and experiencing flak as God's kingdom advances. Your group might like to share bread and wine together as you pray for one another, reading Matthew 26:26–29 before you do so.

Notes

Leader's Notes

WEEK ONE: Who is the King?

Opening Exercise
Just as the Fatherhood of God can be difficult for those who've had bad human fathers, so most of us have picked up warped ideas about power, authority and kingship. We're going to be looking at the King and His kingdom over the next seven weeks. This is a good opportunity to bring any wrong thinking or attitudes into the open and shed a bit of light on them.

Aim of the Session
If this is a new group, introduce people and agree some ground rules, then start the study. To understand the kingdom we need to know the King. We're trying to understand: what kind of a king is Jesus? What does He expect of us and what can we expect of Him? What can we learn, for example, about control issues in our own lives, from the way He exercises authority?

The skilful way in which curators place pictures next to one another helps my understanding of art exhibitions enormously. Adjacent works throw light on each other – through contrast, similarity or allusion. Juxtaposition of scriptures from different parts of the Bible can have a similar effect – which is why I've included a number of different readings here. You don't have to use all of them. As mentioned in the Introduction, it would be invaluable if people read through the whole of Matthew before embarking on this study guide. A mere glance at some of the readings each week may then be enough to remind you.

I've started this study of authority and the kingdom in Matthew's Gospel by looking at the King. God has always been King, though fallen angels and human beings still try to usurp His authority. But what kind of King is God – is Jesus? Matthew's very Judaic Gospel demonstrates how Jesus fulfilled everything God wanted for His chosen people. Genealogies in Matthew trace Jesus' human ancestry. They emphasise Abraham (he fathered a nation whose King was God) and David – Israel's great human king, who sinned and repented. Jesus is 'great David's greater Son'. They emphasise the Exile, arising from Israel's rebellion against God's authority. The genealogies mention some less than glorious characters, who were nevertheless part of God's plan – isn't that encouraging?! Finally God sent His 'Anointed One'.

This Gospel – and hence this Study Guide – is very challenging. People experiencing high challenge with low support can become defensive or anxious, even hostile. The disciples had high support, from Jesus in the flesh. We have the Holy Spirit and one another. As leader, do discern and intervene should individuals feel condemned as hopeless cases, rather than convicted by the Holy Spirit about something specific that needs repentance and change.

I've aimed to make the Discussion Starters as practical and life-related as possible. Jesus said there is no point in hearing His words, then failing to act on them. Agreeing to keep personal matters confidential within the group will help to encourage honest responses. If you find the group coming out with stock, 'safe Christian' answers you'll need to pray – and challenge them. Praying with and supporting one another will also help teaching become practice. If this means taking two weeks or

LEADER'S NOTES

more on each session, so be it – this isn't a quick 'course' with an exam to cram for at the end. Christian teaching takes time to work from our heads to our hearts and lives – and for this process we need both grace and truth.

WEEK TWO: Kingdom in Contention

Opening Exercise
Encourage honesty here but also some good practical kingdom thinking. Or, if you're considering the Personal Application section as a group, you might want to wait until later. One example of practical kingdom thinking about conflict came from a man in my church homegroup who found himself having to make a difficult phone call to someone at work. He prayed before dialling and felt God was telling him to smile – and to keep smiling. 'I found that it's almost impossible to lose your rag when you're smiling benevolently at someone, even if you can't see them,' he said. The conflict was resolved amicably; my friend has discovered a good strategy.

Aim of the Session
To help and equip people to 'fight the good fight' in a godly way.

Last session we looked at the King: for the rest of the sessions we are looking at the kingdom. It's simple – where God is given power and authority – but also complex – think how often Jesus needed to say, 'The kingdom of God/heaven is like…'. Though we are looking at different aspects of the kingdom in different sessions, they all overlap. Do glance through the headings and Bible passages of other sessions, since you may well find discussion veering off into areas that we'll be looking at later. Try to deflect these. I started with this 'contention' aspect of the kingdom mainly to follow the chronology in Matthew. I sense Christ's temptations tested the way in which He would establish the kingdom even more than they tested Him as an individual.

In the last part of Discussion Starter 2, try not to get bogged down in how much Jesus knew and how much things were predestined or at risk according to His response etc. He 'emptied himself' and was 'tempted as we are', so I believe the faith and hope (and even knowledge?) available to Him was not so different from that available to us.

You might find it helpful to use a commentary alongside this book. Tom Wright's *Matthew for Everyone* (in two paperback volumes, SPCK, 2002) makes the best of modern scholarship highly accessible – and relates Bible teaching to today. One of the most difficult (and important) passages we're looking at this week is Matthew 5:38–42. Understanding the background, Tom Wright makes the point that, in that setting, you would have been struck on the right cheek with the back of the right hand – in other words this was not about physical violence but about trading (or refusing to trade) insults. The word translated 'resist' in verse 39 (NIV) comes from a Greek word – arraying armies against each other. Be aware, when discussing Discussion Starter 7 that bullying, domestic violence and abuse are widespread but often kept hidden. Someone within your group, or someone close to them, may be suffering in silence and Jesus' words, taken at face value, may be inappropriate advice. It's nevertheless true that the kingdom's growth, from the cross onwards, has been fed by the blood of the martyrs.

WEEK THREE: Radically Different Power and Authority – The Good News of the Kingdom

Opening Exercise
After everyone has shared briefly which news item affected them the most, get them to count up – how many were items of good news and how many of bad? Try to draw out that we need to be aware of what is going on so we can pray and act, as there's no merit in burying our heads in the sand. On the other hand, kingdom people are gospel (or good news) people and

LEADER'S NOTES

maybe we should also expect the good news of the kingdom to be in our minds and on our lips. Even at times when defeats and bad news abound, Jesus is beautiful!

Aim of the Session
The aim in this session is to explore the question, 'What's so good about this kingdom?' If we're meant to be extending God's kingdom by spreading the good news about it, we'll need to understand the answer! There's such challenge here that we'll need to find ways of accessing God's grace and goodness – and find encouragement, prayer and support from one another.

Each week some of the Discussion Starters may be more appropriate to your group than others, and there are lots of readings – you may or may not want to use them all. They are bound to raise interesting and possibly important questions about all kinds of details, but try to keep discussion to this week's topic, since other aspects of the huge subject of the kingdom will be covered in future weeks.

Matthew 9–10 gives examples of the kind of authority that Jesus exercised – and expected His disciples to exercise. They also suggest the opposition to be expected as kingdoms clash. Though chapter and verse numbers were later additions, sometimes we stop reading at the end of one chapter, which means that we may miss something vital. Jesus told His disciples to pray to the Lord of the harvest, 'to send out workers into his harvest field' (9:38). The next sentence (10:1) has Jesus calling the Twelve, giving them authority to heal and deliver – and then He sends them out in answer to their own prayer!

Matthew 11:2–6 echoes Isaiah 61:1–3, which Jesus used as the manifesto of His ministry and of the kingdom (see Luke 4).

Tom Wright translates the NIV's word 'blessed' in Matthew 5:3–12 as 'wonderful news for...'. Some of Jesus' requirements later in the same chapter sound less than wonderful news!

Discussion Starter 4: According to Scripture, a woman made 'unclean' through permanent vaginal bleeding was cut off from religious observance – and touching her should have contaminated Jesus. The good news was that the reverse happened – His touch healed her, freeing her to worship and to re-establish human contact.

Discussion Starter 6: You might want to look at Romans 14:17.

WEEK FOUR: Growth – The Subversive Secret of the Kingdom

Opening Exercise
If you're going to cook bread, work out the timings to see whether you'll need to start the dough off early. Rolls will cook quicker than a large loaf. Bread-making machines have rapid one-hour programmes but are less 'hands-on'.

If bread-making is impractical, try this instead. You'll need a small cake and a couple of those trick child's birthday-party candles that re-light after they are blown out. The cake is to celebrate 2,000+ years of the kingdom. Ask people what they think its secret ingredient might be.

Get someone to light the candles as you tell how Jesus brought the light of the kingdom into the world. When He died the light seemed to go out (get someone to blow out the candles). As they light again, talk about the resurrection and growth of the Church (you might want to sing a song of praise together) but then the terrible persecutions which drove it underground. (Candles blown out again.) But the Church survived and grew stronger than ever. (You could sing praises again.) Heresies threatened it. Dark hours came – the Inquisition, the Crusades, the suppression of the Scriptures, totalitarian atheist governments... Finally you'll need to extinguish the candles by

LEADER'S NOTES

holding them under water – but nothing can extinguish the kingdom's life, not even death!

Aim of the Session
This session is all about getting more excited about the subversive secret of God's kingdom. To understand that we're a bit like agents in a war-time setting who need to count the cost, but also to understand our Leader's strategy, to adjust ourselves to His thinking and His ways and to recognise the surprising weapons at our disposal.

Discussion Starter 1: Be sensitive. You may find people express their emotions about shattered dreams and long-unanswered prayers. The Bible is full of such – but, rather than jumping in with quick-fix solutions or Bible verses, it might be appropriate for the group to hold someone's pain and stand with them. God can defend Himself, as well as being, finally, our Rock!

Discussion Starter 2: For example, nowhere does the Bible condemn slavery, yet the 'yeast' of the kingdom eventually worked on Christians until some fought to have it abolished, with much hard-won success in their generation (although it's not eradicated yet).

Discussion Starter 3: I've sat through hours of complex teaching on how to communicate the gospel in a post-modern society. It boils down to this – communicate through stories, pictures, actions and small groups. Jesus knew a thing or two!

Discussion Starter 4: A quick internet search will find how Gandhi, Martin Luther King and others effectively utilised non-violence.

WEEK FIVE: Upside-down Kingdom

Opening Exercise
When people brought their complaints before God in psalms of lament they were often blisteringly honest, bringing their grievances into His presence, into the Temple, into their worship. We don't do this very regularly. Yet often God would give lamenting psalmists a new perspective on the situation; their complaints turned to praise as He turned their thinking and attitude upside down.

You might also try to encourage people who wrote about unfair things that worked to their disadvantage to think of instances which show the other side of the coin. Thank God that the justice for which He cares so passionately differs so much from our idea of fairness.

Aim of the Session
'To the Jews who had believed him, Jesus said, "If you hold to my teaching, you are really my disciples. Then you will know the truth, and the truth will set you free"' (John 8:31–32). If people grasp, and live, the truth of what we're looking at in this session – the utterly surprising and super-abundant grace of God – it could not only set individuals free but turn the world upside down!

I smiled at a T-shirt that read, 'Jesus loves you – but I'm his favourite'. Isn't that just the silly way we think sometimes? Grace doesn't work like that though. It can be a double-edged sword. If we accept it for ourselves, we must accept that God will lavish it on others too – and that's the challenge of some of the Discussion Starters. For example, it's not fair that those who work for two minutes are paid the same as those who work twelve hours in the vineyard – except that all agreed to work for that wage and any boss is entitled to be generous if he wants. If we struggle with these unfairness issues, we're like insecure children within a family or like Jesus' early disciples who vied

LEADER'S NOTES

for position (Matt. 20:21–22). We may need not only a healthy dollop of truth but an even bigger one of grace to live it out. We love because He first loved us!

Discussion Starter 1: Obviously every church will need to find wisdom in setting and patrolling 'boundaries' and observe safeguarding protocols rigorously.

Discussion Starter 2: One important point is that children are happy to receive, while adults, especially rich ones, like to be self-sufficient. Citizens of the kingdom aren't self-sufficient.

WEEK SIX: Kingdom Citizens' Responsibilities

Opening Exercise
Depending on the size of your group, you may need to limit this to a quick 'best and worst thing'. Encourage them to think about concrete details – we often cope with the big issues and fall down on the little ones.

We need each other as we worship, since no one person has a full picture of God. If we each bring our piece of the jigsaw, something that is special to us as individuals, it can be very powerful. As 1 Corinthians 14:26 instructs, 'When you come together, each of you has a hymn, or a word of instruction, a revelation, a tongue or an interpretation. Everything must be done so that the church may be built up.'

Aim of the Session
The way citizens of the kingdom treat one another – and the rest of God's children – takes up so much space in the Bible that it's clearly of paramount importance to God. You'll only scratch the surface in this session and it may not feel safe or comfortable. For those who subscribe to the 'individual is king' mentality, however, this could be life-changing!

There are some hard words concerning judgment in some of this week's Bible passages. It would be good for the group to talk over individuals' fears and hopes and help one another avoid misunderstandings.

Discussion Starter 2: In his story *The Visit* (illustrated edition, HarperCollins Religious, 1999), or in *The Final Boundary* (Kingsway Publications, 1987) Adrian Plass imagined the effect it would have on a church community if Jesus came for a while among them in the flesh. Reading an extract from one of these theological fantasies could help 'earth' some of your discussions. They also reveal the humour and compassion found in many of the challenges that can seem stark when Jesus isn't with us in the flesh.

Discussion Starter 3: The fish appear in Matthew 13:47–49.

Discussion Starter 5: This has proved contentious in church history, so make sure people apply kingdom attitudes as they discuss it! You might like to look again at Matthew 23:13–15, a serious warning against the abuse of spiritual power.

WEEK SEVEN: Laying Hold of the Kingdom

Opening Exercise
Here are some ideas that I thought of: acorns, love (from its first stage of romantic attraction, then commitment in marriage, continued loving when things are not so good, even beyond the grave), an idea for a novel, business or invention... Tensions might stem from impatience or lack of understanding of different timescales – making it hard to hold on when things are tough and easy to lose hope when progress seems to be backwards.

We're living in God's kingdom, but it is a kingdom that is still going through birth pangs. Like a woman in labour, we feel the strain and the tension – bringing to birth, creating, is often painful.

LEADER'S NOTES

Aim of the Session
Understanding that we need to be real about living 'in the world but not of it'. Aim to count the cost, to understand the tensions and the need to encourage one another. Then seek new faith in God and the power of Christ's resurrection. Remember that His faith in us is an essential part of His plan to see His kingdom come.

Discussion Starter 6: Different people-groups are not necessarily those who live the other side of the world. They are many groups of people who speak the same language and have the same culture – maybe those who congregate at the local golf club – or rave venue! Of course, with the growing number of refugees, many will find different cultures and people-groups right on our doorsteps.

Having reached the end of this Study Guide, it would be good to take stock. So often we say, 'Done that!' having studied one piece of Christian teaching and rush on to another, without taking time to let either affect us. Or perhaps they do affect us – making us feel even more inadequate than we did before! We've heard the teaching, we know what's right now, but should we not be putting it into practice?

So, what have people learned from this study of the kingdom in Matthew? You may have gained some head knowledge but what impact has it made on individuals' lives – and on the life of the group? It would be good to spend time talking through the practical ways in which you are working this out. Pray for one another. Listen out too for anyone who is finding the challenge too great. The starting place for this kingdom is the foot of the cross, where we come with nothing. There we receive Christ's love – and then the power of His resurrection so we can live this kingdom life. And when we mess it up, we can come back to the cross, again and again. What other lord, what other king, would allow that?

Daily Guide

This Daily Guide is designed to help you to engage with the material in the Study Guide between the sessions. More copies of this daily guide are available to download for free from **wvly.org/c2ccv**.

Day 1	Complete Week 1 in the Study Guide.
Day 2	Read Matthew 8, with authority in mind.
Day 3	Prayer for the day: Teach me to understand and follow Your authority.
Day 4	Action – Spend 15 minutes reading some of Matthew afresh, as though you were there.
Day 5	Read Matthew 21.
Day 6	Prayer for the day: Hold before God someone on your heart who is in authority and others oppressed by it.
Day 7	Action – Look for opportunities to show someone how radical Jesus' authority is.
Day 8	Complete Week 2 in the Study Guide.
Day 9	Read Matthew 4.
Day 10	Prayer for the day: Thank you Jesus for Your integrity, humility and authority that attracts people to follow You and also shows up evil for what it is.

Day 11	Action – Pray for attitudes of love, humility and understanding, check facts, then write to someone in power with your concerns about an oppressed people.
Day 12	Read Matthew 13:24–43.
Day 13	Prayer for the day: Thank you God that, in the end, You, not we, will judge – justly and with mercy.
Day 14	Action – Ask the Holy Spirit to show you where you are judgemental, especially of people in church. Maybe apologise? Pray that church leaders will exercise authority under God's wisdom and guidance.
Day 15	Complete Week 3 in the Study Guide.
Day 16	Read Matthew 5.
Day 17	Prayer for the day: Thank you, Lord, for the good news of Your kingdom. Help me understand and live within it more.
Day 18	Action – Think of someone you want to bless. Seek for special blessing from God for them. Tell them.
Day 19	Read Matthew 9:1–10:8.
Day 20	Prayer for the day: Lord, show me to whom to go in Your name, with Your good news.
Day 21	Action – Do what God told you yesterday.
Day 22	Complete Week 4 in the Study Guide.
Day 23	Read Matthew 13.
Day 24	Prayer for the day: Lord when I don't understand Your pace or way of working, encourage me with glimpses of growth in Your kingdom.
Day 25	Action – 'Tell the truth but tell it slant' (Emily Dickinson.) Tell a fable; paint, post or wear something that will intrigue people about eternal matters.
Day 26	Read Matthew 6.
Day 27	Prayer for the day: Lord, may people see You in me, through actions and attitudes as well as words.

DAILY GUIDE

Day 28 Action – Spend some time in the secret place with God, simply listening, accepting His love and letting Him fill you with Himself.

Day 29 Complete Week 5 in the Study Guide.

Day 30 Read Matthew 19:13 – 20:16.

Day 31 Prayer for the day: Lord, when Scriptures throw me off balance or seem unfair, help me know Your heart and change my mind-set.

Day 32 Action – If God challenged you through anything in the reading, try to act on what He's saying.

Day 33 Read Matthew 22:1–10.

Day 34 Prayer for the day: Lord, show me which seemingly unlikely person You're wanting to invite to your banquet.

Day 35 Action – Extend Jesus' invitation to that person.

Day 36 Complete Week 6 in the Study Guide.

Day 37 Read Matthew 18.

Day 38 Prayer for the day: Lord, help me not to cause others to stumble and to forgive any who harm me.

Day 39 Action – Who sits uncomfortably on the edge of your church or community? Reach out, include and value them.

Day 40 Read Matthew 7:24–29 and 16:13–20.

Day 41 Prayer for the day: Lord, help me to put into practice Your words and Your teaching.

Day 42 Action – If Jesus is truly your rock, are you prepared, like Peter, to be a rock on which He builds a bit of his kingdom? Is anything holding you back?

Day 43 Complete Week 7 in the Study Guide.

The Cover to Cover Bible Study Series

CHARACTERS

Abraham
Adventures of faith
ISBN: 978-1-78259-089-7

Barnabas
Son of encouragement
ISBN: 978-1-85345-911-5

David
A man after God's own heart
ISBN: 978-1-78259-444-4

Elijah
A man and his God
ISBN: 978-1-85345-575-9

Elisha
A lesson in faithfulness
ISBN: 978-1-78259-494-9

Jacob
Taking hold of God's blessing
ISBN: 978-1-78259-685-1

Joseph
The power of forgiveness and reconciliation
ISBN: 978-1-85345-252-9

Mary
The mother of Jesus
ISBN: 978-1-78259-402-4

Moses
Face to face with God
ISBN: 978-1-85345-336-6

THEMES

Bible Genres
Hearing what the Bible really says
ISBN: 978-1-85345-987-0

Covenants
God's promises and their relevance today
ISBN: 978-1-85345-255-0

The Creed
Belief in action
ISBN: 978-1-78259-202-0

The Divine Blueprint
God's extraordinary power in ordinary lives
ISBN: 978-1-85345-292-5

Fruit of the Spirit
Growing more like Jesus
ISBN: 978-1-85345-375-5

God's Rescue Plan
Finding God's fingerprints on human history
ISBN: 978-1-85345-294-9

Great Prayers of the Bible
Applying them to our lives today
ISBN: 978-1-85345-253-6

The Holy Spirit
Understanding and experiencing Him
ISBN: 978-1-85345-254-3

The Image of God
His attributes and character
ISBN: 978-1-85345-228-4

Names of God
Exploring the depths of God's character
ISBN: 978-1-85345-680-0

NEW: Revival
Seeking and encountering abundant life
ISBN: 978-1-78951-441-4

Rivers of Justice
Responding to God's call to righteousness today
ISBN: 978-1-85345-339-7

The Second Coming
Living in the light of Jesus' return
ISBN: 978-1-85345-422-6

The Uniqueness of our Faith
What makes Christianity distinctive?
ISBN: 978-1-85345-232-1

NEW: Violence against Women
Discovering El Roi, The God Who Sees
ISBN: 978-1-78951-445-2

NEW TESTAMENT

NEW: Matthew
Your Kingdom Come
ISBN: 978-1-78951-450-6

Mark
Life as it is meant to be lived
ISBN: 978-1-85345-233-8

Luke
A prescription for living
ISBN: 978-1-78259-270-9

John's Gospel
Exploring the seven miraculous signs
ISBN: 978-1-85345-295-6

Acts 1–12
Church on the move
ISBN: 978-1-85345-574-2

Acts 13–28
To the ends of the earth
ISBN: 978-1-85345-592-6

The Letter to the Romans
Good news for everyone
ISBN: 978-1-85345-250-5

1 Corinthians
Growing a Spirit-filled church
ISBN: 978-1-85345-374-8

2 Corinthians
Restoring harmony
ISBN: 978-1-85345-551-3

Galatians
Freedom in Christ
ISBN: 978-1-85345-648-0

Ephesians
Claiming your inheritance
ISBN: 978-1-85345-229-1

Philippians
Living for the sake of the gospel
ISBN: 978-1-85345-421-9

The Letter to the Colossians
In Christ alone
ISBN: 978-1-855345-405-9

Thessalonians
Building Church in changing times
ISBN: 978-1-78259-443-7

1 Timothy
Healthy churches – effective Christians
ISBN: 978-1-85345-291-8

2 Timothy and Titus
Vital Christianity
ISBN: 978-1-85345-338-0

Philemon
From slavery to freedom
ISBN: 978-1-85345-453-0

Hebrews
Jesus – simply the best
ISBN: 978-1-85345-337-3

James
Faith in action
ISBN: 978-1-85345-293-2

1 Peter
Good reasons for hope
ISBN: 978-1-78259-088-0

2 Peter
Living in the light of God's promises
ISBN: 978-1-78259-403-1

1,2,3 John
Walking in the truth
ISBN: 978-1-78259-763-6

Revelation 1–3
Christ's call to the Church
ISBN: 978-1-85345-461-5

Revelation 4–22
The Lamb wins! Christ's final victory
ISBN: 978-1-85345-411-0

The Armour of God
Living in His strength
ISBN: 978-1-78259-583-0

The Beatitudes
Immersed in the grace of Christ
ISBN: 978-1-78259-495-6

The Lord's Prayer
Praying Jesus' way
ISBN: 978-1-85345-460-8

Parables
Communicating God on earth
ISBN: 978-1-85345-340-3

Prayers of Jesus
Hearing His heartbeat
ISBN: 978-1-85345-647-3

The Prodigal Son
Amazing grace
ISBN: 978-1-85345-412-7

The Sermon on the Mount
Life within the new covenant
ISBN: 978-1-85345-370-0

OLD TESTAMENT

Genesis 1–11
Foundations of reality
ISBN: 978-1-85345-404-2

Genesis 12–50
Founding fathers of faith
ISBN: 978-1-78259-960-9

Exodus
God's Epic Rescue
ISBN: 978-1-78951-272-4

The Ten Commandments
Living God's Way
ISBN: 978-1-85345-593-3

Joshua 1–10
Hand in hand with God
ISBN: 978-1-85345-542-7

Joshua 11–24
Called to service
ISBN: 978-1-78951-138-3

Judges 1–8
The spiral of faith
ISBN: 978-1-85345-681-7

Judges 9–21
Learning to live God's way
ISBN: 978-1-85345-910-8

Ruth
Loving kindness in action
ISBN: 978-1-85345-231-4

Nehemiah
Principles for life
ISBN: 978-1-85345-335-9

Esther
For such a time as this
ISBN: 978-1-85345-511-7

Job
The source of wisdom
ISBN: 978-1-78259-992-0

Psalms
Songs of life
ISBN: 978-1-78951-240-3

23rd Psalm
The Lord is my shepherd
ISBN: 978-1-85345-449-3

Proverbs
Living a life of wisdom
ISBN: 978-1-85345-373-1

Ecclesiastes
Hard questions and spiritual answers
ISBN: 978-1-85345-371-7

Song of Songs
A celebration of love
ISBN: 978-1-78259-959-3

Isaiah 1–39
Prophet to the nations
ISBN: 978-1-85345-510-0

Isaiah 40–66
Prophet of restoration
ISBN: 978-1-85345-550-6

Jeremiah
The passionate prophet
ISBN: 978-1-85345-372-4

Ezekiel
A prophet for all times
ISBN: 978-1-78259-836-7

Daniel
Living boldly for God
ISBN: 978-1-85345-986-3

Hosea
The love that never fails
ISBN: 978-1-85345-290-1

Joel
Getting real with God
ISBN: 978-1-78951-927-2

Jonah
Rescued from the depths
ISBN: 978-1-78259-762-9

Habakkuk
Choosing God's way
ISBN: 978-1-78259-843-5

Haggai
Motivating God's people
ISBN: 978-1-78259-686-8

Zechariah
Seeing God's bigger picture
ISBN: 978-1-78951-263-2

For current prices or to order, visit **waverleyabbeytrust.org/publishing**